Master Maths at Home

Fractions, Decimals, Percentage and Ratio

Scan the QR code to help your child's learning at home.

mastermathsathome.com

How to use this book

Maths — No Problem! created Master Maths at Home to help children develop fluency in the subject and a rich understanding of core concepts.

Key features of the Master Maths at Home books include:

- Carefully designed lessons that provide structure, but also allow flexibility in how they're used.

- Speech bubbles containing content designed to spark diverse conversations, with many discussion points that don't have obvious 'right' or 'wrong' answers.

- Rich illustrations that will guide children to a discussion of shapes and units of measurement, allowing them to make connections to the wider world around them.

- Exercises that allow a flexible approach and can be adapted to suit any child's cognitive or functional ability.

- Clearly laid-out pages that encourage children to practise a range of higher-order skills.

- A community of friendly and relatable characters who introduce each lesson and come along as your child progresses through the series.

You can see more guidance on how to use these books at **mastermathsathome.com**.

We're excited to share all the ways you can learn maths!

Copyright © 2022 Maths — No Problem!

Maths — No Problem!
mastermathsathome.com
www.mathsnoproblem.com
hello@mathsnoproblem.com

First published in Great Britain in 2022 by
Dorling Kindersley Limited
One Embassy Gardens, 8 Viaduct Gardens, London SW11 7BW
A Penguin Random House Company

The authorised representative in the EEA is Dorling Kindersley
Verlag GmbH. Arnulfstr. 124, 80636 Munich, Germany

10 9 8 7 6 5 4 3 2 1
001–327109–May/22

A CIP catalogue record for this book is available from the British Library.

ISBN: 978-0-24153-953-8
Printed and bound in the UK

For the curious
www.dk.com

This book was made with Forest Stewardship Council™ certified paper – one small step in DK's commitment to a sustainable future. For more information go to www.dk.com/our-green-pledge

Acknowledgements
The publisher would like to thank the authors and consultants Andy Psarianos, Judy Hornigold, Adam Gifford and Dr Anne Hermanson.

The Castledown typeface has been used with permission from the Colophon Foundry.

Contents

Ruby Elliott Amira Charles Lulu Sam Oak Holly Ravi Emma Jacob Hannah

Simplifying fractions

Starter

Hannah, Amira and Ruby each bought the same chocolate bar.

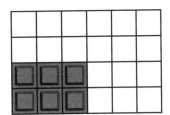 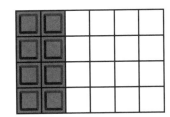 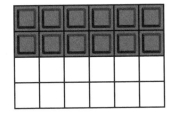

 I ate 18 pieces.

 I ate 16 pieces.

 I ate 12 pieces.

Can you show what fraction they each ate in the simplest form?

Example

 Each chocolate bar had 24 pieces to begin with.

Dividing the numerator and the denominator by their highest common factor gives us the fraction in its simplest form.

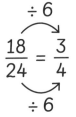 Hannah ate $\frac{18}{24}$ of her bar, Amira ate $\frac{16}{24}$ of her bar and Ruby ate $\frac{12}{24}$ of her bar.

The highest common factor for 18 and 24 is 6.

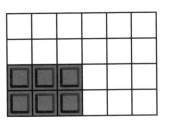

$$\frac{18}{24} \overset{\div 6}{\underset{\div 6}{=}} \frac{3}{4}$$

4

The highest common factor for 16 and 24 is 8.

The highest common factor for 12 and 24 is 12.

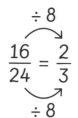

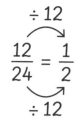

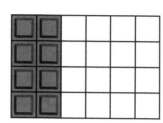

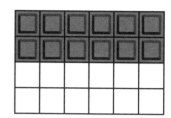

Hannah ate $\frac{3}{4}$ of her bar, Amira ate $\frac{2}{3}$ of her bar and Ruby ate $\frac{1}{2}$ of her bar.

Practice

1 Circle the fractions written in their simplest form.

$\frac{21}{35}$

$\frac{2}{3}$

$\frac{5}{7}$

$\frac{27}{33}$

2 Write each fraction in their simplest form.

(a) $\frac{14}{21} = \dfrac{\square}{\square}$

(b) $\frac{15}{27} = \dfrac{\square}{\square}$

(c) $\frac{24}{64} = \dfrac{\square}{\square}$

(d) $\frac{56}{72} = \dfrac{\square}{\square}$

Comparing fractions

A cafe recorded how many eggs it used over 3 days in a table.
On which day did the cafe use the greatest number of eggs?
On which day did it use the smallest number of eggs?

Day	Cartons of eggs used
Monday	$2\frac{3}{4}$ cartons of eggs
Tuesday	$2\frac{5}{6}$ cartons of eggs
Wednesday	$\frac{7}{2}$ cartons of eggs

Example

Compare the fractions.

$\frac{7}{2} > 3$

$2\frac{3}{4} < 3$

$2\frac{5}{6} < 3$

$\frac{7}{2}$ is the greatest fraction because it is the only fraction greater than 3.

$\frac{7}{2} = 3\frac{1}{2}$

We can find the common denominator for $\frac{3}{4}$ and $\frac{5}{6}$.
Twelfths are common to both quarters and sixths.

$2\frac{3}{4} = 2\frac{9}{12}$ $2\frac{5}{6} = 2\frac{10}{12}$

$2\frac{9}{12} < 2\frac{10}{12}$

We can use diagrams to compare fractions.

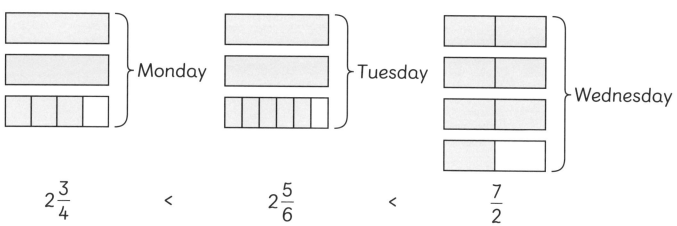

$2\dfrac{3}{4}$ < $2\dfrac{5}{6}$ < $\dfrac{7}{2}$

The cafe used the greatest number of eggs on Wednesday and the smallest number of eggs on Monday.

Practice

1 Put the fractions in order from smallest to greatest.

$3\dfrac{3}{5}$ $3\dfrac{1}{2}$ $3\dfrac{3}{10}$

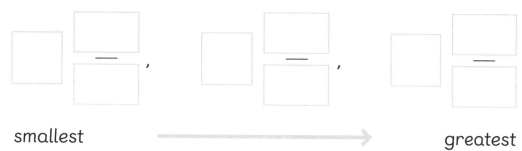

smallest   ⟶   greatest

2 Put the fractions in order from greatest to smallest.

$1\dfrac{3}{8}$ $1\dfrac{3}{4}$ $1\dfrac{1}{2}$

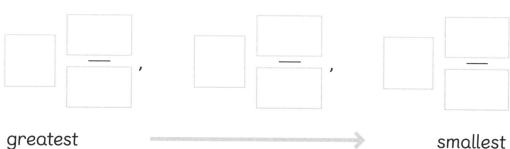

greatest   ⟶   smallest

Adding and subtracting fractions (part 1)

Starter

Amira helped her dad wash his car.
Amira's dad poured $\frac{1}{2}$ l of water and $\frac{1}{3}$ l of detergent into a bucket to make a cleaning solution. When they finished, there was $\frac{1}{4}$ l of cleaning solution remaining in the bucket.
How much cleaning solution did they use to wash the car?

Example

Find out how much cleaning solution Amira and her dad started with.

$\frac{1}{2} + \frac{1}{3} = ?$

We need to find a smaller piece that both $\frac{1}{2}$ and $\frac{1}{3}$ can be broken into so we can add them together.

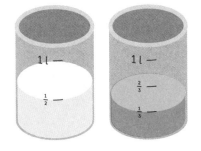

The smaller piece is a **common multiple** of both 2 and 3.

$2 \times 3 = 6$
Halves and thirds can both be broken into sixths.

$\frac{1}{2}$

$\frac{3}{6}$

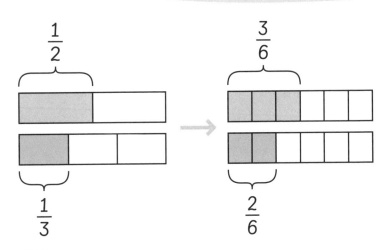

$\frac{1}{3}$

$\frac{2}{6}$

$$\frac{3}{6}$$ + 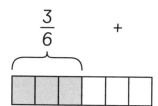 $$\frac{2}{6}$$ 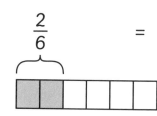 = $$\frac{5}{6}$$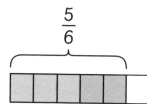

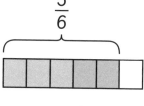

They started with $\frac{5}{6}$ l of cleaning solution.

Subtract $\frac{1}{4}$ from $\frac{5}{6}$.

$$\frac{5}{6}$$ $$\frac{1}{4}$$

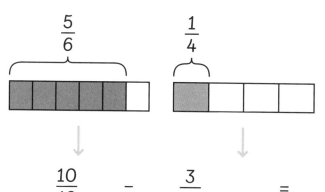

$4 \times 6 = 24$

I can use twenty-fourths but 12 is the lowest common multiple of both 6 and 4 so I will use twelfths.

$$\frac{10}{12}$$ − $$\frac{3}{12}$$ = $$\frac{7}{12}$$

Amira and her dad used $\frac{7}{12}$ l of cleaning solution to clean the car.

Practice

1 Add.

(a) $\frac{1}{2} + \frac{1}{4} = $ ☐

(b) $\frac{1}{2} + \frac{3}{8} = $ ☐

(c) $\frac{2}{5} + \frac{2}{3} = $ ☐

(d) $\frac{5}{6} + \frac{1}{8} = $ ☐

2 Subtract.

(a) $\frac{3}{4} - \frac{1}{2} = $ ☐

(b) $\frac{3}{4} - \frac{5}{8} = $ ☐

(c) $\frac{5}{7} - \frac{1}{4} = $ ☐

(d) $\frac{5}{6} - \frac{3}{4} = $ ☐

Adding and subtracting fractions (part 2)

Starter

In the morning, a baker has 1 kg of flour. He uses $\frac{1}{2}$ kg of the flour to bake a loaf of bread. He then uses $\frac{3}{8}$ kg of the flour to bake some rolls. In the afternoon, he goes to a shop and purchases $1\frac{3}{4}$ kg more flour. How much flour does the baker have now?

Example

After using $\frac{1}{2}$ kg of flour, the baker is left with $\frac{1}{2}$ kg of flour.

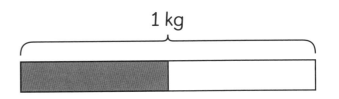

1 kg

$$1 = \frac{2}{2}$$

$$\frac{2}{2} - \frac{1}{2} = \frac{1}{2}$$

We can only add and subtract fractions if the denominators are the same. We need to find a **common denominator**. Halves, quarters and eighths can all be changed to eighths.

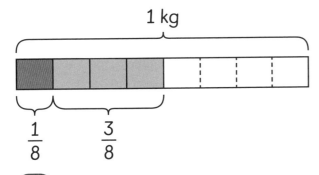

1 kg

$\frac{1}{8}$ $\frac{3}{8}$

$$\frac{1}{2} = \frac{4}{8}$$

$$\frac{4}{8} - \frac{3}{8} = \frac{1}{8}$$

To subtract $\frac{3}{8}$ from $\frac{1}{2}$, first change $\frac{1}{2}$ to $\frac{4}{8}$.

Next, add $1\frac{3}{4}$ to $\frac{1}{8}$.
We need all the denominators to be eighths.

 + 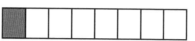 =

$1\frac{3}{4} = 1\frac{6}{8}$

$1\frac{6}{8} + \frac{1}{8} = 1\frac{7}{8}$

The baker now has $1\frac{7}{8}$ kg of flour.

Practice

1 Add.

(a) $\frac{7}{8} + \frac{1}{4} = $

(b) $1\frac{1}{2} + \frac{3}{8} = $

(c) $2\frac{5}{6} + 3\frac{3}{4} = $

(d) $\frac{8}{3} + 1\frac{3}{4} = $

2 Subtract.

(a) $\frac{7}{9} - \frac{2}{3} = $

(b) $1\frac{3}{8} - \frac{1}{4} = $

(c) $7\frac{1}{2} - 3\frac{7}{8} = $

(d) $\frac{31}{20} - 1\frac{2}{5} = $

Multiplying fractions (part 1)

Starter

Lulu and her family drank some fizzy water with their lunch. Lulu and her older sister drank $\frac{1}{2}$ of a $\frac{3}{4}$-l bottle of fizzy water. Lulu's mum drank $\frac{2}{3}$ of a $\frac{3}{4}$-l bottle of fizzy water.

How much fizzy water did Lulu and her older sister drink?
How much fizzy water did Lulu's mum drink?

Example

First, let's work out how much fizzy water Lulu and her older sister drank.

This represents 1 l.

The shaded part represents $\frac{3}{4}$.

The bottle holds $\frac{3}{4}$ l of fizzy water.

We write $\frac{1}{2}$ of $\frac{3}{4}$ as $\frac{1}{2} \times \frac{3}{4}$.

$\frac{1}{2} \times \frac{3}{4} = \frac{3}{8}$

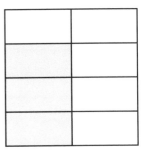

$\frac{2}{3} \times \frac{3}{4} = \frac{6}{12}$

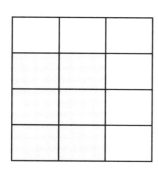

Lulu's mum drank $\frac{2}{3}$ of a $\frac{3}{4}$-l bottle of fizzy water.

We write this as $\frac{2}{3} \times \frac{3}{4}$.

$\frac{6}{12} = \frac{1}{2}$

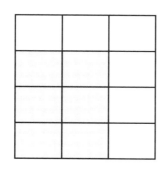

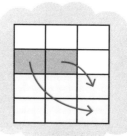

Lulu and her older sister drank $\frac{3}{8}$ l of fizzy water.

Lulu's mum drank $\frac{1}{2}$ l of fizzy water.

Practice

Find the product.

1 $\frac{1}{2} \times \frac{3}{5} = \boxed{} \; \frac{}{}$

2 $\frac{3}{5} \times \frac{1}{2} = \boxed{} \; \frac{}{}$

3 $\frac{1}{4} \times \frac{1}{3} = \boxed{} \; \frac{}{}$

4 $\frac{1}{2} \times \frac{2}{3} = \boxed{} \; \frac{}{}$

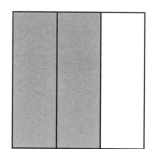

Multiplying fractions (part 2)

Starter

Amira and Ravi are walking to school. Amira lives $\frac{4}{5}$ of a kilometre away from school. She still has $\frac{1}{4}$ of the distance to walk. Ravi lives $\frac{2}{5}$ of a kilometre away from the school. He still has $\frac{1}{2}$ of the distance to walk.

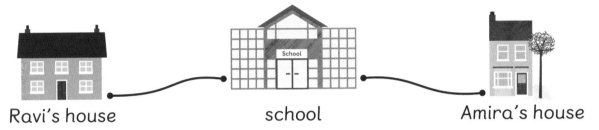

Ravi's house   school   Amira's house

Who is closer to school?

Example

> We can use bars to help us.

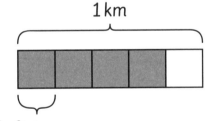

1 km

left to go

$$\frac{1}{4} \times \frac{4}{5} = \frac{1}{5}$$

> Each piece is $\frac{1}{5}$.
> $\frac{1}{4}$ of 4 pieces is 1 piece.

> Each piece is $\frac{1}{5}$.
> $\frac{1}{2}$ of 2 pieces is 1 piece.

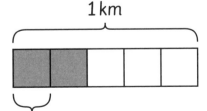

1 km

left to go

$$\frac{1}{2} \times \frac{2}{5} = \frac{1}{5}$$

$\frac{1}{2}$ of $\frac{2}{5}$ is equal to $\frac{1}{4}$ of $\frac{4}{5}$.

$$\frac{1}{2} \times \frac{2}{5} = \frac{1}{{}_2\cancel{4}} \times \frac{{}^2\cancel{4}}{5}$$

We can also multiply fractions this way.

First, we multiply the numerators. Next, we multiply the denominators.

$$\frac{1}{4} \times \frac{4}{5} = \frac{1 \times 4}{4 \times 5} \qquad \frac{1}{2} \times \frac{2}{5} = \frac{1 \times 2}{2 \times 5}$$

$$\frac{1 \times 4}{4 \times 5} = \frac{4}{20} \qquad \frac{1 \times 2}{2 \times 5} = \frac{2}{10}$$

We can then find the simplest forms of the fractions.

$$\overset{\div 4}{\frac{4}{20}} = \frac{1}{5} \qquad \overset{\div 2}{\frac{2}{10}} = \frac{1}{5}$$
$$\underset{\div 4}{} \qquad \underset{\div 2}{}$$

Amira and Ravi are both $\frac{1}{5}$ of a kilometre away from school.

Practice

Find the product.

1 $\frac{1}{3} \times \frac{3}{7} =$ ☐ ——— ☐

2 $\frac{2}{5} \times \frac{5}{9} =$ ☐ ——— ☐

3 $\frac{1}{6} \times \frac{3}{5} =$ ☐ ——— ☐

 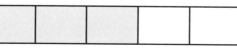

4 $\frac{1}{2} \times \frac{5}{7} =$ ☐ ——— ☐

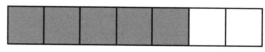

Dividing fractions

Starter

Five sixths of a pizza is shared equally between some friends.
What fraction of the whole pizza does each friend get if there are 5 friends?
How about if there are 3 friends?

Example

There are 5 pieces of pizza. Each piece is $\frac{1}{6}$ of the whole pizza.

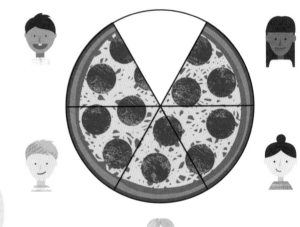

If 5 friends share the pizza equally, each friend gets 1 slice.

$$\frac{5}{6} \div 5 = \frac{1}{6}$$

We can also say that each friend gets $\frac{1}{5}$ of $\frac{5}{6}$ of a whole pizza.

$$\frac{1}{5} \times \frac{5}{6} = \frac{1}{6}$$

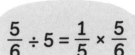

$$\frac{5}{6} \div 5 = \frac{1}{5} \times \frac{5}{6}$$

If 5 friends share $\frac{5}{6}$ of a whole pizza equally, each friend gets $\frac{1}{6}$ of the whole pizza.

If 3 friends are sharing, everyone can get 1 whole piece. That leaves 2 pieces.

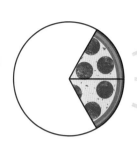

To share the 2 remaining pieces, we can cut each of them into 3 smaller pieces. Each one of the smaller pieces is $\frac{1}{18}$ of the whole pizza.

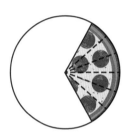

 $\frac{1}{6}$ = $\frac{3}{18}$

The friends also get 2 of those smaller pieces.

 $\frac{3}{18}$
 $\frac{2}{18}$

Each friend gets $\frac{3}{18} + \frac{2}{18}$ of the whole pizza.

$$\frac{3}{18} + \frac{2}{18} = \frac{5}{18}$$

 $\frac{3}{18}$
 $\frac{2}{18}$

 $\frac{3}{18}$
 $\frac{2}{18}$

$$\frac{5}{6} \div 3 = \frac{15}{18} \div 3$$

$$\frac{15}{18} \div 3 = \frac{5}{18}$$

If 3 friends share $\frac{5}{6}$ of a whole pizza equally, each friend gets $\frac{5}{18}$ of the whole pizza.

1 Fill in the blanks.

(a) $\frac{1}{2} \div 2 = \dfrac{\boxed{}}{\boxed{}}$

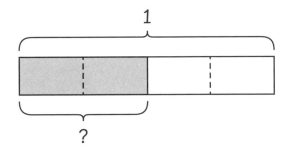

(b) $\frac{1}{2} \div 4 = \dfrac{\boxed{}}{\boxed{}}$

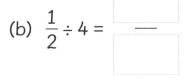
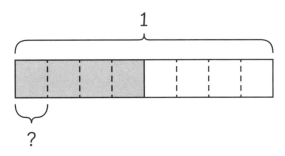

(c) $\frac{1}{2} \div 6 = \dfrac{\boxed{}}{\boxed{}}$

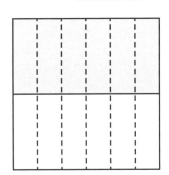

(d) $\frac{1}{2} \div 5 = \dfrac{\boxed{}}{\boxed{}}$

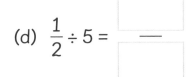
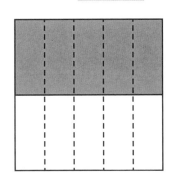

(e) $\frac{3}{4} \div 3 = \dfrac{\boxed{}}{\boxed{}}$

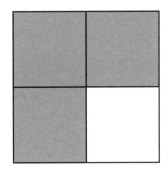

(f) $\frac{3}{4} \div 2 = \dfrac{\boxed{}}{\boxed{}}$

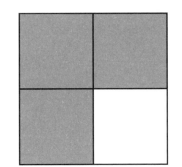

(g) $\dfrac{6}{7} \div 3 = \dfrac{\boxed{}}{\boxed{}}$

(h) $\dfrac{7}{8} \div 14 = \dfrac{\boxed{}}{\boxed{}}$

(i) $\dfrac{3}{5} \div 2 = \dfrac{3}{5} \times \dfrac{1}{2} = \dfrac{\boxed{}}{\boxed{}}$

(j) $\dfrac{2}{3} \div 3 = \dfrac{2}{3} \times \dfrac{1}{\boxed{}} = \dfrac{\boxed{}}{\boxed{}}$

2 Draw a bar model and fill in the blanks.

A waiter needs to share $\dfrac{3}{4}$ l of chilli sauce equally between 6 bottles.

What fraction of a litre should the waiter pour in each bottle?

The waiter should pour $\dfrac{\boxed{}}{\boxed{}}$ l in each bottle.

Multiplying decimals

Starter

Amira is helping her mum bake mince pies for the school holiday bake sale. Amira's mum has four 0.454 kg packs of butter. How much butter does she have in total?

Example

Multiply 4 by 0.454 to work out how much butter Amira's mum has in total.

?

0.454 kg

Multiplying decimals is like multiplying whole numbers. We need to be careful to write the numbers in the correct columns.

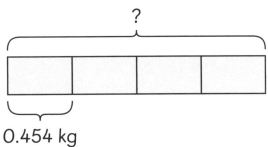

$$
\begin{array}{r}
0 \,.\, 4 \ \overset{1}{5} \ 4 \\
\times \qquad\quad 4 \\
\hline
6 \\
\hline
\end{array}
$$

$$
\begin{array}{r}
0 \,.\, \overset{2}{4} \ \overset{1}{5} \ 4 \\
\times \qquad\quad 4 \\
\hline
1 \ 6 \\
\hline
\end{array}
$$

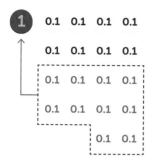

0.1 0.1 0.1 0.1
0.1 0.1 0.1 0.1
0.1 0.1 0.1 0.1
0.1 0.1 0.1 0.1
0.1 0.1

$$\begin{array}{r}
{}^{1}0 . {}^{2}4 \ {}^{1}5 \ 4 \\
\times \qquad\qquad 4 \\
\hline
8 \ 1 \ 6 \\
\hline
\end{array}$$

1
0.1 0.1 0.1 0.1
0.1 0.1 0.1 0.1

0.01 0.001 0.001 0.001 0.001
0.001 0.001

$$\begin{array}{r}
{}^{1}0 . {}^{2}4 \ {}^{1}5 \ 4 \\
\times \qquad\qquad 4 \\
\hline
1 . 8 \ 1 \ 6 \\
\hline
\end{array}$$

Amira's mum has 1.816 kg of butter in total.

Practice

Find the product.

1
$$\begin{array}{r}
6 . 3 \ 5 \\
\times \qquad 4 \\
\hline
\end{array}$$

2
$$\begin{array}{r}
1 . 1 \ 2 \ 5 \\
\times \qquad\qquad 8 \\
\hline
\end{array}$$

3
$$\begin{array}{r}
5 . 0 \ 2 \ 1 \\
\times \qquad 1 \ 5 \\
\hline
\end{array}$$

4
$$\begin{array}{r}
2 . 7 \ 1 \ 2 \\
\times \qquad 1 \ 9 \\
\hline
\end{array}$$

Fractions as decimals

Starter

A shopkeeper needs to divide 5 kg of rice into 8 jars equally.

How much rice does the shopkeeper need to put into each jar?

Example

I think we can draw bar models to help us.

$1 \div 8 = \frac{1}{8}$

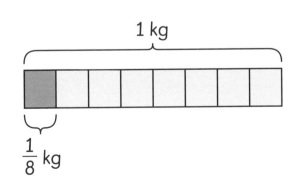

1 kg

$\frac{1}{8}$ kg

1 kg

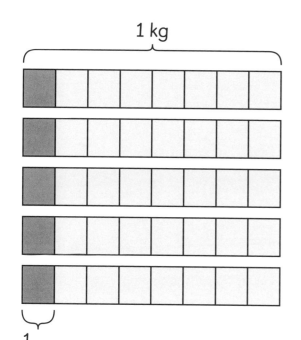

$\frac{1}{8}$ kg

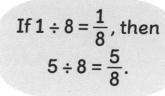
If $1 \div 8 = \frac{1}{8}$, then
$5 \div 8 = \frac{5}{8}$.

The shopkeeper needs to put $\frac{5}{8}$ kg of rice into each jar.

Measuring scales only show weight in decimals. We need to convert $\frac{5}{8}$ into a decimal.

We can divide 5 by 8 to find out how much should go into each jar.

We can use long division to help us.

Be careful to write the numbers in the correct columns when dividing.

```
        0 . 6   2   5
   8 )  5 . 0   0   0
      - 4 . 8   0   0
        0 . 2   0   0
      - 0 . 1   6   0
        0 . 0   4   0
      - 0 . 0   4   0
        0 . 0   0   0
```

$8 > 5$
I know that the answer is less than 1.

$\frac{5}{8}$ is equal to 625 thousandths.
$\frac{5}{8} = \frac{625}{1000} = 0.625$

We can also convert kilograms to grams. There are 1000 g in 1 kg. We can say that 1 g is 1 thousandth of a kg.

```
        6   2   5
8 ) 5   0   0   0
  - 4   8   0   0
        2   0   0
  -     1   6   0
            4   0
  -         4   0
             0
```

$5 \div 8 = \dfrac{5}{8} = 0.625$

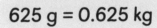

5 kg = 5000 g
We can divide 5000 by 8 to find out how many grams go into each jar.

625 g = 0.625 kg

The shopkeeper needs to put 0.625 kg of rice into each jar.

Practice

1 Convert the proper fractions into decimals.

(a) $\dfrac{1}{4} = 0.$ ☐

(b) $\dfrac{1}{8} = 0.$ ☐

(c) $\dfrac{3}{4} = 0.$ ☐

(d) $\dfrac{2}{5} = 0.$ ☐

(e) $\dfrac{7}{8}$ = 0. ☐

(f) $\dfrac{3}{40}$ = 0. ☐

2 Show each number as a fraction in its simplest form.

(a) 0.9 = $\dfrac{\boxed{}}{\boxed{}}$

(b) 0.47 = $\dfrac{\boxed{}}{\boxed{}}$

(c) 0.75 = $\dfrac{\boxed{}}{\boxed{}}$

(d) 0.125 = $\dfrac{\boxed{}}{\boxed{}}$

(e) 0.875 = $\dfrac{\boxed{}}{\boxed{}}$

(f) 0.257 = $\dfrac{\boxed{}}{\boxed{}}$

Rounding recurring decimals

I need to put $\frac{2}{3}$ of the flour into 1 bowl and the other $\frac{1}{3}$ of the flour into a different bowl.

1.000 kg

How much flour does Oak need to put into each bowl?

Example

Let's divide 1 by 3 to find $\frac{1}{3}$ and 2 by 3 to find $\frac{2}{3}$.

I can keep dividing and get more decimal places with the same number each time. The equivalent decimal of $\frac{1}{3}$ is a recurring decimal.

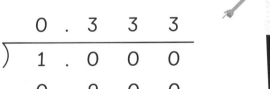

$$
\begin{array}{r}
0.333 \\
3\,\overline{)\,1.000} \\
-\,0.900 \\
\hline
0.100 \\
-\,0.090 \\
\hline
0.010 \\
-\,0.009 \\
\hline
0.001
\end{array}
$$

My scale only shows 3 decimal places. I can round $\frac{1}{3}$ to 0.333.

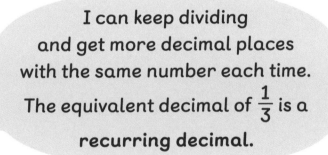

We say $\frac{1}{3} \approx 0.333$.

If I keep dividing 2 by 3, I also get a recurring decimal.

I can round $\frac{1}{3}$ to 0.667.

We say $\frac{2}{3} \approx 0.667$.

```
        0 . 6   6   6
  3 )   2 . 0   0   0
    -   1 . 8   0   0
        0 . 2   0   0
    -   0 . 1   8   0
        0 . 0   2   0
    -   0 . 0   1   8
        0 . 0   0   2
```

Oak needs to put approximately 0.333 kg of flour into 1 bowl and approximately 0.667 kg into a different bowl.

Practice

Convert the fractions to their decimal equivalents.
Round to 3 decimal places.

1 $\frac{1}{3} =$ ☐

2 $\frac{2}{3} =$ ☐

3 $\frac{5}{6} =$ ☐

4 $\frac{1}{9} =$ ☐

5 $\frac{5}{9} =$ ☐

6 $\frac{7}{9} =$ ☐

Percentages of numbers

Starter

There are 540 pupils at Douglas Fir Primary School.
60% of the pupils walk to school every day.

How many pupils walk to Douglas Fir Primary School every day?

Example

To find 60% of 540, we can first find 10% of 540.

540

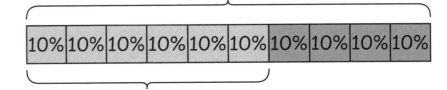

| 10% | 10% | 10% | 10% | 10% | 10% | 10% | 10% | 10% | 10% |

?

$540 \div 10 = 54$

10% of 540 is 54.

$54 \times 6 = 324$

60% of 540 is 324.

324 pupils walk to Douglas Fir Primary School every day.

Practice

1 An airline keeps track of the age of the passengers on their flights.
The table below shows the ages of the last 7000 passengers.
Complete the table.

Age of passengers	Percentage of passengers	Number of passengers
< 15 years old	15%	
15–65 years old	80%	
> 65 years old	5%	

2 Ravi's parents want to buy a new sofa.
They like both the Plush and Opulent sofas.
Which sofa costs more after the discounts are applied?
How much more?

Plush Sofa £1154 — sale! Take 20% off the price.

Opulent Sofa £1270 — sale! Take 30% off the price.

The [   ] sofa costs £ [   ] more than the

[   ] sofa after the discounts are applied.

Percentages of quantities

Charles buys a box of 80 red and blue pens
for the school maths club.
The label on the box states that
20% of the pens are red.
How many red pens are there in the box?

Example

We can use
bars to help us.

First, we
can find 10% of 80.
$80 \div 10 = 8$
10% of 80 is 8.

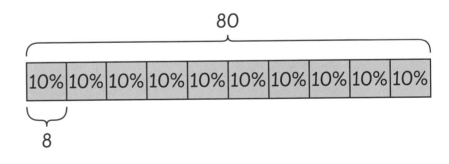

80

| 10% | 10% | 10% | 10% | 10% | 10% | 10% | 10% | 10% | 10% |

8

If 10% of
80 is 8, then 20%
of 80 is 16.

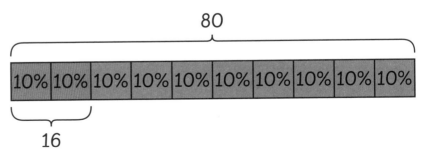

80

| 10% | 10% | 10% | 10% | 10% | 10% | 10% | 10% | 10% | 10% |

16

30

I can see that 20% of 80 is the same as $\frac{1}{5}$ of 80.

$\frac{1}{5} = 1 \div 5 = 0.2 = \frac{20}{100}$

$\frac{20}{100} = 20\%$

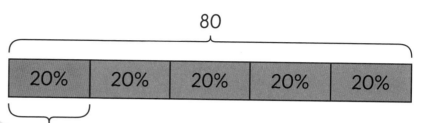

80

| 20% | 20% | 20% | 20% | 20% |

16

There are 16 red pens in the box.

Practice

1 Fill in the blanks.

(a) 10% of 750 ml = ⬚ ml

(b) 25% of £248 = £ ⬚

(c) 50% of 1.684 km = ⬚ km

(d) 17% of 400 kg = ⬚ kg

2 Draw a bar model to solve the problem and fill in the blanks.
Holly had £120 of savings. She spent 20% of her savings on some new shoes. She then spent 50% of her remaining savings on some clothes. How much did the clothes cost?
How much money did Holly have left?

The clothes cost £ ⬚ .

Holly had £ ⬚ left.

Percentages as increases or decreases

Starter

Lulu and Ravi are making photo albums for their families. The photos they have are all 80 mm wide. They want the head shots to be 20 mm wide and the other photos to be 120 mm wide.

We need to reduce the head shots by 80% and enlarge the other photos by 120%.

I don't agree. Reducing the head shots by 80% will make the head shots too small, but enlarging the other photos by 120% will not make them large enough.

Who is correct?

Example

reduce

20 mm

To reduce means to decrease the size of the photo.

80 mm

enlarge →

80 mm

120 mm

To enlarge means to increase the size of the photo.

Let's start with the enlargements first.

We need to increase the size of a photo by 40 mm to make it 120 mm wide.

80 mm

100%

If 100% is 80 mm, what percentage is 40 mm?

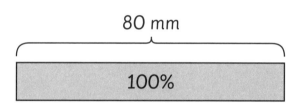

80 mm   40 mm

100%   ?

120 mm

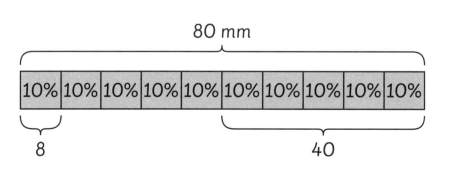

80 mm

| 10% | 10% | 10% | 10% | 10% | 10% | 10% | 10% | 10% | 10% |

8   40

10% of 80 is 8.
50% of 80 is 40.

100% + 50% = 150%

80 mm | 40 mm

| 100% | 50% |

120 mm

The photos need to be enlarged to 150% of their original size.

$150\% = \dfrac{150}{100} = 1.5$

We can check by multiplying 80 by 1.5.

$80 \times 1.5 = 120$

$120 \div 80 = 1.5$
$1.5 = 150\%$

We need to reduce the head shots so they are 20 mm wide.

50% of 80 mm is 40 mm.
25% of 80 mm is 20 mm.
The head shots need to be reduced to 25% of their original size.

80 mm

| 25% | 25% | 50% |

20   40

We can check by multiplying 80 by 0.25.
$80 \times 0.25 = 20$

$20 \div 80 = 0.25$
$0.25 = 25\%$

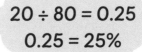

Ravi is correct.

They need to reduce the head shots by 75% to make the head shots 25% of their original size.

The other photos need to be enlarged by 150% to make them 150% of their original size.

1 Elliott's cat weighs 20% as much as Elliott. Altogether, they weigh 48 kg. How much does each of them weigh?

Elliott weighs [ ] kg and his cat weighs [ ] kg.

2 Elliott's dog weighs 25% as much as Elliott.
How much does Elliott's dog weigh?
How much does Elliott, his cat and his dog weigh altogether?

Elliott's dog weighs [ ] kg.

Altogether, Elliott, his cat and his dog weigh [ ] kg.

Percentages as a comparison

Starter

I have 150 points. I have 20% more points than Sam.

I have 120 points. I have 25% less points than Jacob.

Is this possible?

Example

I don't think it's possible.

I think it is possible. 25% of one number can be equal to 20% of a different number.

150

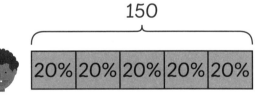

| 20% | 20% | 20% | 20% | 20% |

| 25% | 25% | 25% | 25% | 25% |

120

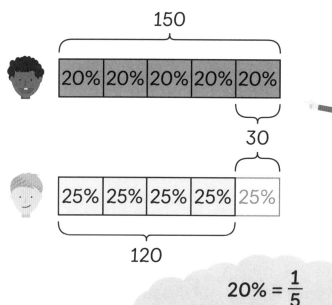

To find 20% of 150, we can multiply 150 by 0.2.
150 × 0.2 = 30

To find 25% of 120, we can multiply 120 by 0.25.
120 × 0.25 = 30

$20\% = \frac{1}{5}$

$25\% = \frac{1}{4}$

20% of 150 = 25% of 120

It is possible.
20% of 150 and 25% of 120 are both 30.

Practice

Draw a bar model and fill in the blanks.
Ravi has 200% as much money as Charles has. Ruby has 50% as much money as Charles has.
Ruby's money is equal to what percentage of Ravi's money?

Ruby's money is equal to ☐ % of Ravi's money.

Ratio: comparing quantities

Starter

A box of ice cream cones is packed with 3 vanilla ice cream cones and 2 chocolate ice cream cones. How can we compare the number of vanilla and chocolate ice cream cones in the box?

Example

There is one fewer 🍦 than 🍦. There are 50% more 🍦 than 🍦.

There are $\frac{2}{3}$ as many 🍦 than 🍦.

For every 2 🍦 there are 3 🍦.

We call this **ratio**. We can write the ratio as 2 : 3. We say there is a ratio of '2 to 3'.

The ratio of to 🍦 is 2 : 3.

Each breakfast set in a restaurant comes with the same items.

strawberries

eggs

slices of toast

melon slices

Fill in the blanks.

1 The ratio of eggs to slices of toast is ☐ : ☐ .

2 The ratio of slices of toast to eggs is ☐ : ☐ .

3 The ratio of strawberries to melon slices is ☐ : ☐ .

4 The ratio of strawberries to eggs is ☐ : ☐ .

Ratio: comparing numbers

Starter

On Wednesday, the science museum sold 254 more child tickets than adult tickets. For every 3 adults that visited the science museum, there were 5 children that visited. How many people visited the science museum on Wednesday altogether?

Example

We can start by drawing a model to show the ratio of 3 : 5 for adults to children.

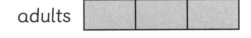

adults

children

Next, we can show the difference of 254.
254 ÷ 2 = 127

adults

children | 127 | 127 |

254

Each part of the model has a value of 127. Now we can work out how many people visited the science museum.
127 × 8 = 1016

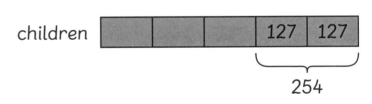

adults | 127 | 127 | 127 |

children | 127 | 127 | 127 | 127 | 127 |

1016 people visited the science museum on Wednesday altogether.

1 Draw a model to solve the problem.
The ratio of Jacob's weight to his dog's weight is 3 : 2. Together, they weigh 60 kg.
How much do Jacob and his dog each weigh?

Jacob weighs ☐ kg and his dog weighs ☐ kg.

2 Fill in the blanks and solve.

Ravi is setting the table for dinner. He needs 1 fork and 1 knife for each place.

He uses $\frac{1}{3}$ of the knives and $\frac{1}{5}$ of the forks to set 8 places.

How many forks and knives does he have left?

Ravi has ☐ forks left and ☐ knives left.

Review and challenge

1 Match the equivalent fractions.

$\dfrac{15}{40}$ •   • $\dfrac{3}{8}$

$\dfrac{14}{21}$ •   • $\dfrac{6}{7}$

$\dfrac{10}{16}$ •   • $\dfrac{2}{3}$

$\dfrac{18}{21}$ •   • $\dfrac{5}{8}$

2 Put the fractions in order from greatest to smallest.

$2\dfrac{1}{2}$ $2\dfrac{4}{7}$ $2\dfrac{5}{8}$

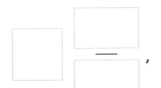 ,  ,

greatest ⟶ smallest

3 Fill in the blanks.

(a) $3\dfrac{1}{3} + 4\dfrac{5}{6} =$

(b) $\dfrac{8}{5} + 1\dfrac{3}{4} =$

(c) $6\dfrac{1}{2} - 6\dfrac{3}{8} =$

(d) $\dfrac{35}{15} - 1\dfrac{2}{5} =$

4 Find the product.

(a) $\frac{1}{3} \times \frac{3}{4} = \boxed{}$

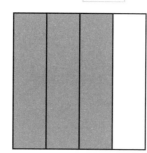

(b) $\frac{3}{5} \times \frac{5}{6} = \boxed{}$

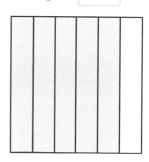

5 One third of the pupils from Evergreen School took part in a maths competition. The pupils were put into 4 equal groups.

(a) What fraction of the $\frac{1}{3}$ of Evergreen School pupils that took part are in each group?

(b) What fraction of all the Evergreen School pupils are in each group?

(c) If there are 22 pupils in each group, how many pupils go to Evergreen School?

6 $\frac{3}{4}$ l of water is poured equally into 8 glasses.

How much water is poured into each glass?

$\boxed{}$ l of water is poured into each glass.

7 There are 260 pupils at Elmgrove Primary School.

260

60% of all the pupils at Elmgrove Primary School have at least one pet.
The table shows information about the pets they have.

Pets	Percentage of pupils at Elmgrove Primary School
dog	30%
cat	25%
more than one pet	15%
one pet but not a cat or a dog	5%

(a) ☐ pupils have at least one pet.

(b) There are (more / fewer) pupils with no pets than pupils with a dog as a pet.

(c) ☐ more pupils have (dogs / cats) than have (dogs / cats) as a pet.

(d) There are ☐ pupils without any pets.

(e) There are ☐ fewer pupils with pets that are not cats or dogs than there are pupils with more than one pet.

8 In the first year of opening, a music shop started selling a new electric guitar. In the second year, the music shop increased the price of the electric guitar by 10%. In the third year, it increased the price of the electric guitar by 10% of the second year price.

The price of the electric guitar in the third year was ⬚ % more than its price in the first year.

9 A film darkroom technician needs to mix a solution of film developer. The table shows the ratio of all the chemicals required to mix different amounts of film developer.
Complete the table for the technician.

Developer solution	Number of parts required	To mix 1 l (ml)	To mix 5 l (ml)	To mix 20 l (l)
water	5	500		10
developer part A	2	200		
developer part B	2			
activator	1	100		

Answers

Page 5 **1** $\boxed{\frac{21}{35}}$ $\left(\frac{2}{3}\right)$ $\left(\frac{5}{7}\right)$ $\boxed{\frac{27}{33}}$ **2** (a) $\frac{14}{21} = \frac{2}{3}$ (b) $\frac{15}{27} = \frac{5}{9}$ (c) $\frac{24}{64} = \frac{3}{8}$ (d) $\frac{56}{72} = \frac{7}{9}$

Page 7 **1** $3\frac{3}{10}, 3\frac{1}{2}, 3\frac{3}{5}$ **2** $1\frac{3}{4}, 1\frac{1}{2}, 1\frac{3}{8}$

Page 9 **1** (a) $\frac{1}{2} + \frac{1}{4} = \frac{3}{4}$ (b) $\frac{1}{2} + \frac{3}{8} = \frac{7}{8}$ (c) $\frac{2}{5} + \frac{2}{3} = 1\frac{1}{15}$ (d) $\frac{5}{6} + \frac{1}{8} = \frac{23}{24}$ **2** (a) $\frac{3}{4} - \frac{1}{2} = \frac{1}{4}$ (b) $\frac{3}{4} - \frac{5}{8} = \frac{1}{8}$ (c) $\frac{5}{7} - \frac{1}{4} = \frac{13}{28}$

(d) $\frac{5}{6} - \frac{3}{4} = \frac{1}{12}$

Page 11 **1** (a) $\frac{7}{8} + \frac{1}{4} = 1\frac{1}{8}$ (b) $1\frac{1}{2} + \frac{3}{8} = 1\frac{7}{8}$ (c) $2\frac{5}{6} + 3\frac{3}{4} = 6\frac{7}{12}$ (d) $\frac{8}{3} + 1\frac{3}{4} = 4\frac{5}{12}$ **2** (a) $\frac{7}{9} - \frac{2}{3} = \frac{1}{9}$ (b) $1\frac{3}{8} - \frac{1}{4} = 1\frac{1}{8}$

(c) $7\frac{1}{2} - 3\frac{7}{8} = 3\frac{5}{8}$ (d) $\frac{31}{20} - 1\frac{2}{5} = \frac{3}{20}$

Page 13 **1** $\frac{1}{2} \times \frac{3}{5} = \frac{3}{10}$ **2** $\frac{3}{5} \times \frac{1}{2} = \frac{3}{10}$ **3** $\frac{1}{4} \times \frac{1}{3} = \frac{1}{12}$ **4** $\frac{1}{2} \times \frac{2}{3} = \frac{1}{3}$

Page 15 **1** $\frac{1}{3} \times \frac{3}{7} = \frac{1}{7}$ **2** $\frac{2}{5} \times \frac{5}{9} = \frac{2}{9}$ **3** $\frac{1}{6} \times \frac{3}{5} = \frac{1}{10}$ **4** $\frac{1}{2} \times \frac{5}{7} = \frac{5}{14}$

Page 18 **1** (a) $\frac{1}{2} \div 2 = \frac{1}{4}$ (b) $\frac{1}{2} \div 4 = \frac{1}{8}$ (c) $\frac{1}{2} \div 6 = \frac{1}{12}$ (d) $\frac{1}{2} \div 5 = \frac{1}{10}$ (e) $\frac{3}{4} \div 3 = \frac{1}{4}$ (f) $\frac{3}{4} \div 2 = \frac{3}{8}$

Page 19 (g) $\frac{6}{7} \div 3 = \frac{2}{7}$ (h) $\frac{7}{8} \div 14 = \frac{1}{16}$ (i) $\frac{3}{5} \div 2 = \frac{3}{5} \times \frac{1}{2} = \frac{3}{10}$ (j) $\frac{2}{3} \div 3 = \frac{2}{3} \times \frac{1}{3} = \frac{2}{9}$ **2** The waiter should pour $\frac{1}{8}$ l in each bottle.

Page 21 **1**

```
      ¹6 . ²3  5
  ×          4
  2  5 . 4  0
```

2

```
  ¹1 . ²1  ⁴2  5
×          8
9 . 0  0  0
```

3

```
    5 . ¹0  2  1
×          1  5
  2  5 . 1  0  5
+ 5  0 . 2  1  0
  7  5 . 3  1  5
```

4

```
  ⁶2 . ¹7  ¹1  2
×          1  9
  2  4 . 4  0  8
+ 2  7 . 1  2  0
  5  1 . 5  2  8
```

Page 24 **1** (a) $\frac{1}{4} = 0.25$ (b) $\frac{1}{8} = 0.125$ (c) $\frac{3}{4} = 0.75$ (d) $\frac{2}{5} = 0.4$

Page 25 (e) $\frac{7}{8} = 0.875$ (f) $\frac{3}{40} = 0.075$ **2** (a) $0.9 = \frac{9}{10}$ (b) $0.47 = \frac{47}{100}$ (c) $0.75 = \frac{3}{4}$ (d) $0.125 = \frac{1}{8}$ (e) $0.875 = \frac{7}{8}$

(f) $0.257 = \frac{257}{1000}$

Page 27 **1** $\frac{1}{3} = 0.333$ **2** $\frac{2}{3} = 0.667$ **3** $\frac{5}{6} = 0.833$ **4** $\frac{1}{9} = 0.111$ **5** $\frac{5}{9} = 0.556$ **6** $\frac{7}{9} = 0.778$

Page 29 1

Age of passengers	Percentage of passengers	Number of passengers
< 15 years old	15%	1050
15–65 years old	80%	5600
> 65 years old	5%	350

2 The Plush sofa costs £34.20 more than the Opulent sofa after the discounts are applied.

Page 31 1 (a) 10% of 750 ml = 75 ml **(b)** 25% of £248 = £62 **(c)** 50% of 1.684 km = 0.842 km **(d)** 17% of 400 kg = 68 kg

2

120 − 24 = 96; 50% of 96 = 48; 96 − 48 = 48. The clothes cost £48. Holly had £48 left.

Page 35 1 Elliott weighs 40 kg and his cat weighs 8 kg. **2** Elliott's dog weighs 10 kg. Altogether, Elliott, his cat and his dog weigh 58 kg.

Page 37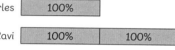

Ruby's money is equal to 25% of Ravi's money.

Page 39 1 The ratio of eggs to slices of toast is 3 : 2. **2** The ratio of slices of toast to eggs is 2 : 3. **3** The ratio of strawberries to melon slices is 4 : 1. **4** The ratio of strawberries to eggs is 4 : 3.

Page 41 1

60 ÷ 5 = 12; 12 × 3 = 36; 12 × 2 = 24. Jacob weighs 36 kg and his dog weighs 24 kg.

2

Ravi has 32 forks left and 16 knives left.

Page 42 1 $\frac{15}{40}$, $\frac{14}{21}$, $\frac{10}{16}$, $\frac{18}{21}$ connected to $\frac{3}{8}$, $\frac{6}{7}$, $\frac{2}{3}$, $\frac{5}{8}$

2 $2\frac{5}{8}$, $2\frac{4}{7}$, $2\frac{1}{2}$ **3 (a)** $3\frac{1}{3} + 4\frac{5}{6} = 8\frac{1}{6}$ **(b)** $\frac{8}{5} + 1\frac{3}{4} = 3\frac{7}{20}$ **(c)** $6\frac{1}{2} - 6\frac{3}{8} = \frac{1}{8}$ **(d)** $\frac{35}{15} - 1\frac{2}{5} = \frac{14}{15}$

Page 43 4 (a) $\frac{1}{3} \times \frac{3}{4} = \frac{1}{4}$ **(b)** $\frac{3}{5} \times \frac{5}{6} = \frac{1}{2}$ **5 (a)** $\frac{1}{4}$ **(b)** $\frac{1}{12}$ **(c)** 264

6 $\frac{3}{4} \div 8 = \frac{3}{32}$. $\frac{3}{32}$ l of water is poured into each glass.

Page 44 7 (a) 156 pupils have at least one pet. **(b)** There are more pupils with no pets than pupils with a dog as a pet. **(c)** 13 more pupils have dogs than have cats as a pet. **(d)** There are 104 pupils without any pets. **(e)** There are 26 fewer pupils with pets that are not cats or dogs than there are pupils with more than one pet.

Answers continued

Page 45 **8**

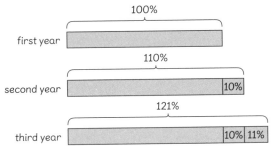

The price of the electric guitar in the third year was 21% more than its price in the first year.

9

Developer solution	Number of parts required	To mix 1 l (ml)	To mix 5 l (ml)	To mix 20 l (l)
water	5	500	2500	10
developer part A	2	200	1000	4
developer part B	2	200	1000	4
activator	1	100	500	2